Art of Getting Money in the 21st Century

Phineas Taylor Barnum

Edward Martins

Legal Notice:

While all attempts have been made to verify information provided in this publication, neither the Author nor the Publisher assumes any responsibility for errors, omissions, or contrary interpretation of the subject matter herein.

This publication is not intended for use as a source of legal or accounting advice. The Publisher wants to stress that the information contained herein may be subject to varying state and/or local laws or regulations. All users are advised to retain competent counsel to determine what state and/or local laws or regulations may apply to the user's particular business.

The Purchaser or Reader of this publication assumes responsibility for the use of these materials and information. Adherence to all applicable laws and regulations, federal, state, and local, governing professional licensing, business practices, advertising, and all other aspects of doing business in the United States or any other jurisdiction is the sole responsibility of the Purchaser or Reader.

The Author and Publisher assume no responsibility or liability whatsoever on the behalf of any Purchaser or Reader of these materials.

Any perceived slights of specific people or organizations are unintentional.

Note:

You may not resell this product or the any of its rights. Every rights are protected.

Contents

Secrets of the Riches 6

What are Riches? 8

Who is Successful? 11

Keys to Success 23

Keys to Grow Rich 35

Focus 35

Confidence 41

Self-Discipline 54

Golden Rules for Making Money 56

About Barnum: 56

Don't Mistake Your Vocation 58

Select The Right Location 61

Avoid Debt 65

Persevere 69

Whatever You Do, Do It With All Your Might 72

Depend Upon Your Own Personal Exertions 74

Don't Get Above Your Business 78

Do Not Scatter Your Powers 86

Be Systematic 87

Beware Of "Outside Operations" 91

Don't Indorse Without Security 93

Advertise Your Business 96

Be Polite And Kind To Your Customers 102

Don't Blab 104

Preserve Your Integrity 105

Internet marketing a big advantage to many businesses..108

Affiliate Marketing 115

Article Marketing 118

E-mail Marketing 121

Blog Marketing 124

Pay-per-click or PPC 126

Search Engine Optimization (SEO) 128
Pop-up Ads 130
Social Media Marketing 133
Mobile Marketing 135

Secrets of the Riches

Would you like to realize your goals? Maybe you'd like to run your own business, expand your material possessions, or succeed in the arts. There is no one path to the pot of gold, but many people of all backgrounds have successfully found it.

Whether you want to follow the ways of the great financiers, the famous politicians, or the dynamic movie stars, there are common modes of behavior each of them followed.

And in many cases, they have shared their secrets so YOU CAN FOLLOW THEIR FOOTSTEPS.

"If you wish to know the road up the mountain, ask the person who goes back and forth on it," said the ancient sage, Zenrin.

What better way is there to know the secrets than to ask those who made it? What goals do you want to achieve? And what amount of effort can you commit?

You may want money for the extra things in life, money to build a corporate empire, or money to support yourself while you pursue the fine arts.

Perhaps you'd like to take the risk to start something new in your life. You may want to open your own business, devote your energies to an artistic career such as acting, or reap the benefits of your yearly endeavors with fabulous vacations several times a year.

What will bring you happiness? The satisfaction of success takes many forms. Not only are people seeking financial fortunes, but also the ancient goal of peace of mind.

Do you worry? You might be concerned about your health or your family's well-being. You may be anxious about the added expenses of education, medical bills, or the steady increase of cost of living.

There are ways out of the endless cycles of worry, stress and anxiety. Right now, you can rise above the whirl of survival to achieve the accomplishments you dream of!

When you're *for-real* ready to put your whole effort into realizing your goals, YOU WILL SUCCEED.

What are Riches?

"Had I but plenty of money, money enough to spare," wrote Robert Browning. And money is the greatest attribute of riches. A universal desire, money is the materialization of riches, the stuff that makes the rest possible.

Are you looking for financial security? For retirement, for education or leisure? Riches are the *overflowing abundance* of material possessions- houses, cars, boats, furnishings- everything you ever wanted.

Centuries ago, Horace wrote, "By right means, if you can, but by any means, make money." For many people it is a path towards happiness, a cure-all for worry and peace of mind.

For others, riches come in the form of satisfaction and personal independence. Satisfaction comes from accomplishment in employment or attaining goals. It is that feeling of contentment and confidence from a good task well done. Riches are closely linked with success.

And with that comes fame and acknowledgment of position. Success might be the feeling of well-being from the rewards of good effort.

Or the enthusiasm and vitality triggered by recognition. "Success is how well I enjoy the minutes," said producer Norman Lear.

Throughout history, the people who lived with riches often achieved them by hard work, diligence and a belief in themselves. For some people, it took courage, genius and stamina.

But for many others, it took nothing special but the desire to turn dreams into reality.

Whether you want millions of dollars, recognition as an artist, or personal freedom, you have the ability to make your life as rich as you want. Think about what you most desire. It may not be hard cash, but what it can buy.

Or, it may be those feelings of inner satisfaction, from creating something beautiful or strong. You may want personal independence from the work week, or freedom to live anywhere you want.

You may be looking for something meaningful and significant in life- something other than things money can buy.

Whatever your goals, and however difficult they seem to be to accomplish, you have the ability to become who you want.

Take a look- can you see yourself surrounded by riches? Picture the world open and in front of you, ready to become the form of your dreams, ready to stage your desires. "Why then, the world's mine oyster," wrote Shakespeare, "which I with sword will open."

Who is Successful?

Many people who achieve fortune in the world are not born rich. But they accomplished it through hard work and a *plan of action*.

Every type of person on earth can become successful. There are saints and scoundrels; philanthropists and thieves; poets and politicians; young and old. There are no limitations or physical boundaries for success.

Success comes to those who deeply think about success and constantly strive for it!

Although many rich financiers at the turn of the century had no formal education, they overcame that and went on to great fame.

Some people strive towards a single goal from early in life, and often attain that goal while still young. Others are willing to risk new adventures later and still attain success.

"It's never too late to learn," wrote Malcolm Forbes, the money magnate. "I learned to ride a motorcycle at 50 and fly balloons at 52."

Whatever your task, whatever your obstacles, you can be as

successful as anyone else. Study the people who accomplished recognition in the areas of your pursuit. How did they achieve their goals? And don't be afraid you don't have what it takes.

As Daniel Webster wrote, "There is always room at the top."

Forming Conviction-

The single attribute that every successful person has is the one-pointed devotion to attain a goal.

"There in the sunshine are my highest aspirations," wrote Louisa May Alcott, "I can look up and see their beauty, believe in them, and try to follow where they lead."

What are your desires? How can you form them into definite goals that you can attain?

Lawrence Peter wrote, "If you don't know where you're going, you'll probably end up somewhere else."

Maybe you're studying a craft or skill.

Perhaps you're caught in a rung of the corporate ladder.

Or, you might feel constricted by your family and the environment around you. Which star are you reaching for?

"Ours is a world where people *don't know what they want* and

are willing to go through anything to get it," wrote Don Marquis.

Take the time to think about your own aspirations.

Look inside to find what feels right. Almost everyone entertains the notions of fame and fortune, but put on the 'costume' that fits you.

Conviction requires certain qualities of **action**.

You must be sincere and be willing to assume responsibility. And you need the self-discipline necessary to work towards your goals.

- ✓ Are you prepared to achieve your dreams?

- ✓ Can you form their reality in your mind?

- ✓ Will you devote your entire being to attaining what you want**?!?**

On Your Own-

Most millionaires are non-conformists. So are the most famous actors and actresses; and the most prominent artists. Writers are known for their individual traits and eccentricities.

Your convictions and goals are your own business, even when you find help along the path. Mentors often take people under their wings to nourish and teach. Or spiritual guides will show you the path to attainment. But you're on your own to achieve.

Cultivate a sense of justice and an ability to make decisions.

Cooperate with everybody and develop your own self-respect.

And follow good criticism and advice after you've judged carefully.

J. Paul Getty said, "I advise young millionaires to be skeptical of advice. They should advise themselves; they should form their own opinions."

Lord Byron wrote, "There is rapture on the lonely shore." And if you attain your goals with poise and sincerity, you'll find warmth and love at the top- not the cold loneliness pictured by the jealous.

Put on blinders to negative comments and criticism meant to hurt you.

About the people who criticize, Voltaire wrote, "Never having been able to succeed in the world, they took revenge by speaking ill of it."

Seize the Day!

People are judged by what they think and what they say. But the true measure of their character is what they do. Anyone who has achieved success and fortune in the world has done it by **action**.

William Jennings Bryan wrote, "Destiny is not a matter of chance, it is a matter of <u>choice</u>; it is not a thing to be waited for, it is a thing to be **achieved**."

The choice of the path you follow is often put before you as opportunity. "Few people recognize opportunity," said Cary Grant, "because it comes *disguised* as hard work."

Don't let opportunities slip past while you're still considering them, and create new ones as you see them. "Wise people make more opportunities than they find," said Francis Bacon.

What opportunities can you act upon? Woolworth saw a need for small inexpensive items and opened the chain of stores that grossed billions.

Wrigley started giving gum away as a bonus from a supplies wagon he sold from, and saw the opportunity to make money from the gum that became in high demand.

All successful people the world over have found the opportunities for their own special talents and acted upon those ways to achieve. Why wait for the time to pass? There's never a better time than now.

Lewis Carroll believed as many as *six impossible things* before breakfast. Take your own impossible dreams and make them become reality.

How They Think-

Thousands of potential millionaires are born every year. And making a million dollars is coming closer to everyone's pocket. What advice did the money-makers follow?

Aristotle Onassis worked eighteen hours a day to maintain his fortune. He started as a welder and aimed for the top. "You have to think money day and night," he said, "*you should even dream about it in your sleep.*"

John D. Rockefeller, Jr., said, "I believe in the dignity of labor, whether with head or hand; that the world owes every person an opportunity to make a living."

And J. Paul Getty acknowledged his hard work: "I have no complex about wealth. I have worked hard for my money, producing things people need."

Even Proverbs advises: "In all labor there is profit."

Richard Bach, the author of the best selling "Jonathan Livingston Seagull" wrote, "You are never given a wish without also being given the power to make it true. *You may have to work for it*, however."

The Empress of the British Empire, Queen Victoria, admonished, "We are not interested in the possibilities of defeat."

Do YOU Have What it Takes?

There are qualities of endeavor and achievement that are common to many people who make it to the top. The following questions are a guideline to self-enterprise and attaining your goals.

- ✓ Do you prefer to work for yourself than for others?

- ✓ Are you well-informed on current business and political affairs?

- ✓ Are you a leader?

- ✓ Do you take advantage of opportunities?

- ✓ Do you pay attention to what other people say?

- ✓ Can you finish a job even when it is difficult or

unpleasant?

- ✓ Are you challenged by problems?

- ✓ Do you have a goal you want to achieve?

- ✓ Do you consider other people?

- ✓ Do you strive to attain?

- ✓ Can you obey commands?

- ✓ Can you bounce back after defeat?

- ✓ Do you believe in yourself?

- ✓ Can you stand by your actions in spite of criticism?

- ✓ Can you follow instructions?

- ✓ Can you respond to the needs of others?

- ✓ Will you give credit to others?

- ✓ Can you make your own decisions?

- ✓ Are you determined?

- ✓ Are you ready for success?

Establish a Goal-

What do you want?

> - Are you looking for financial security, professional acknowledgment, spiritual attainment?

> - Do you want to fit better socially, or become more expressive creatively?

Establish the goal that's right for you.

Then turn that goal from a dream into a desire. You want to realize that goal, not just wish for it. Aesop said, "Beware that you do not lose the substance by grabbing at the shadow."

→ *Know exactly what you want, then go for it.*

→ *Don't be tricked by your own procrastination- especially if you want to achieve something artistic.*

The writer Thomas Wolfe wrote, "I had been sustained by that delightful illusion of success which we all have when we dream about the books we are going to write instead of actually doing them.

Now I was face to face with it, and suddenly I realized that I had committed my life and my integrity so irrevocably to this struggle that I must conquer now or be destroyed."

Can you see what you want? If you want the abundance of material wealth that money provides, what goal will give you that money?

- ✓ Do you want the prestige of owning your own business?
- ✓ What business do you want to begin?
- ✓ Where are the opportunities for you?

Talk to everyone in the business you want to join. Make friends in the literary or art societies in your area. Read books and articles about your field of endeavor. How can you attain your goal?

"If you don't want to work, *you have to work to earn enough money so that you don't have to work!*" wrote Ogden Nash. Money makes money; success breeds success.

But not always.

How can you break through those thoughts to help yourself to the rewards?

Henry David Thoreau wrote...

"I have learned this at least by my experiment:

That if you advance confidently in the direction of your dreams, and endeavor to live the life which you imagine, you will meet with success."

Think **BIG** and *passionately* visualize success, consistently and without ceasing:

→ Do you see yourself in a big house?

→ Maybe you picture your artwork hanging in a gallery.

→ Can you feel your book in print and in your hands?

→ How does it feel to be a person of success?!?

Affirm- "To make firm."

Make firm that you are; <u>know</u> that it is in your grasp. That's what the others did, and that's how people make it to the top.

Then get down to basics. **Be precise**. E

Exactly how much money do you want, and by what date?

And exactly what are you going to do to earn that money? Be realistic, but give yourself short-term goals. Write it down.

In six months or one year, you will have how much money. And repeat it until it feels good. Then repeat it twice a day until it swirls in your subconscious, until it becomes your one-pointed goal.

"The goal stands up, the keeper stands up to keep the goal," wrote A.E. Housman.

Keys to Success

- ✓ Make people feel at ease- They will respond to your needs as you respond to theirs.

- ✓ Share the spotlight.

- ✓ Give credit to those who deserve it- and to those who strive.

- ✓ Don't grab praise away from other people

- ✓ Have confidence in your own value.

- ✓ Don't do anything that won't credit your own self-respect.

- ✓ Follow up your actions as they reflect your own self-worth.

Listen well to others' comments. Then weigh your own actions. Cultivate relationships with people who have good and important things to say.

Participate in life.

Be active in business meetings and endeavors; volunteer to be part of organizations and groups. Social interaction will boost your sense of well-being.

Feel worthy of your own goal.

Know that you can attain it and that it is right for you.

Grasp your own challenge.

Don't give yourself impossible goals, but always reach higher.

Relax and be yourself. Each person is different and just as wonderful as the next. Don't be plagued by what you think others think of you.

Don't bathe in success- use it. Once you achieve your first goal, go on to others. Use the money you earn for the rewards you look for. Then go on to the next endeavor.

Be slow to criticize others' achievements. Find out how they did it and learn from them.

Never use subterfuge. Don't go behind someone's back. Speak your mind and earn respect.

Banish negative thoughts and traits. Restructure your life to exclude bad habits.

Believe in yourself and what you are to accomplish. All the power in the world is within you to achieve.

Work Towards Your Goal-

"To get profit without risk, experience without danger, and reward without work, is as impossible as it is to live without being born," wrote A. P. Gouthey. Every person who has attained something worth-while has worked for that goal.

Cary Grant said, "I do believe that people can do practically anything they set out to do if they apply themselves diligently and learn."

Which path is the right way towards your goal? Do you need more education? Do you need a few years experience in your field of business? Maybe you need a teacher or guide to help you practice.

"I have learned that success is to be measured not so much by the position that one has reached, as by the obstacles which are overcome while trying to succeed," wrote Booker T. Washington.

What obstacles are in your way? Consider them as easy to pass through as hurdles are to a champion runner. Take each obstacle as a special challenge placed especially for you.

Approach it with intelligence and courage, then learn what it has to teach.

"Success is a journey," said Ben Sweetland, "not a destination."

For some, the process of attainment is the attainment itself. They move on, keep growing and expanding. There is no still water at the top.

"The message from the moon is that no problem need any longer be considered insoluble," wrote Norman Cousins. And you can attain anything that seems impossible.

If you have a problem that needs to be solved, sit calmly and consider it with a clear mind. Observe all the consequences of the actions- both good and bad. Ponder the paths and actions and contemplate the core of the problem. The solution will appear.

"Ask and it shall be given you; seek and ye shall find; knock and it shall be opened to you for everyone who asketh, receiveth. He that seeketh, findeth and to him that knocketh, it shall be opened."

Tap the inner self and encourage positive actions. With each outgoing breath, release the impossible; at each incoming breath, inhale the attainable. Command the best of yourself, but don't despair from an overused sense of perfection.

What can you learn? And who can teach you? Can you attend classes and seminars from universities near home? Check out books from the libraries and absorb the material. Find a master and become an apprentice.

"Anyone who stops learning is old, whether at twenty or eighty," said Henry Ford. "Anyone who keeps learning stays young. The greatest thing in life is to keep your mind young."

Never stop learning; never stop growing and expanding as a person and in your personal endeavor.

Ask Yourself-

As you consider the success you desire, you need to affirm its possibilities and develop the self-confidence necessary to attain

the goals. Learn to do things well. "If you know how to do one thing well, you can do everything," wrote the philosopher Gurdjieff.

→ Are you ready for success?

→ Is what you are doing now helping you to achieve your goals?

→ Do you weigh the consequences before making a decision?

→ Is this the best use of your time?

→ Do you cooperate with everyone and help cultivate their

best potentials?

→ Are you warm and sincere?

→ Do you have the courage to succeed?

→ Do you have the self-discipline necessary to achieve your goals?

→ Do you have a realistic sense of self-worth?

→ Do you give more than you take?

→ Do you have the courage to fail, and then pick up and try again?

→ Can you assume responsibility without blaming others if things go wrong?

→ Are you strong?

→ Can you be sympathetic to life and its sufferings?

→ Can you say no?

→ Will you follow your convictions and plans to achieve?

→ Do you sincerely want to achieve the goals you have chosen?

Taking Responsibility-

"The price of greatness is responsibility," wrote Winston Churchill. Are you willing to take the responsibility once you attain the success you desire?

"The deepest personal defeat suffered by human beings is constituted by the difference between what one was capable of becoming and what one has in fact become," wrote Ashley Montague. And the greatest tragedy is to become less than your full potential, using less than the abilities you have to work with.

Are you waiting for something to happen? Maybe you're waiting for a job offer, or a promotion. Perhaps you're waiting until you get good enough at a craft or skill. Or are you waiting for the inspiration of creativity to strike your life?

It is up to you to take the actions and be responsible for their consequences. "Our responsibility: every opportunity, an obligation; every possession, a duty," wrote John D. Rockefeller, Jr.

Inspire yourself. Read books that will spurn you to action; talk to people who have the vitality you admire. How would you like to lead your life? And make the changes necessary to be like that. "There is nothing permanent except change," wrote Heraclitus.

What changes do you want to make? What are you waiting for?

Accomplishment-

What actions will take you closer to your goals? Decide upon the steps and write them down. Review them until you feel comfortable with those steps. Then repeat them at least once a day, crossing them off as you accomplish them.

"I believe there is no escape from the rule that We must do many, many little things to accomplish even just one big thing," said James Dupont. "This gives me patience when I need it most."

The most rewarding accomplishments are those that take long to achieve and present difficulties.

It is only through these difficulties that a person can rise above the rest to be the unusual, the outspoken and the well-deserved. As if building a kit, follow your own instructions. Decide your best courses of action and achieve their benefits.

Whether the steps are small or large, make them achievable and then do them. Don't commit yourself to things that you never intend to do.

"Even if you're on the right track, you'll get run over if you just sit there," said Will Rogers. Don't be paralyzed by inaction;

rather act upon your own convictions.

Set yourself up for rewards. Don't give yourself goals that have no feeling of satisfaction or no monetary rewards. If you want to be an artist, be the best and learn from the best.

Don't dwell on imperfections or the awkwardness of unpolished skills.

If you go into business, do it for profit or reinvestment. "In business, the earning of profit is something more than an incident

of success. It is an essential condition of success. Because the continued absence of profit itself spells failure," said Justice Brandeis.

Marchant wrote, "To be a success in business, be daring, be first, be different." Think of ways to achieve the best; formulas to increase productivity or decrease overhead. Profit is your drive.

"Profitability is the sovereign criterion of the enterprise," wrote Peter Drucker. And, profitability is the core of any achievement - whether financial or artistic.

Once you achieve your goals, think of ways to benefit others. "Money-getters are the benefactors of our race," said P.T. Barnum. "To them we are indebted for our institutions of learning, and of art, our academies, colleges and churches."

How can you benefit humankind and still keep enough to fulfill your own desires?

The Hidden Asset-

Not all success can be counted in dollars; not all richness is measured by money. "The great secret of success is to go through

life as a person who never gets used up," said Albert Schweitzer.

"Retire upon yourself and look for the ultimate cause of things inside you."

Look within yourself for the ultimate inspiration, and follow the true feelings you discover. "One of my favorite methods is to whisper," said Alfred Hitchcock. "I've discovered the best work is done with sweet reason."

Act upon your own conscience -that guides; that judges your actions and signals your behavior. "Conscience is the inner voice that warns us that someone may be looking," wrote H.L. Mencken.

Accomplish what you desire; fulfill your inner yearnings. But don't compromise your deepest feelings. "We do our best that we know how at the moment, and if it doesn't turn out, we modify it," said F.D. Roosevelt. Follow the paths that life offers you and live the fullest existence you can.

Take a Look-

Look at yourself and look at those who have succeeded throughout history. Do you have what it takes? Even if you have only a few of the qualities of the other great people, you can achieve your heart's desire.

Reach for the highest, then reach higher. Accomplish your steps one by one on a daily basis, always moving forward, always making progress. Encourage yourself. Insist that you can succeed and affirm these thoughts daily.

Keep a sense of proportion and judge for yourself. Then keep busy at the tasks you've set out to accomplish. What's keeping you? "Genius is one percent inspiration and ninety-nine percent perspiration," said Albert Einstein.

Find inspiration wherever you can. Talk to people; read about people; learn your business or craft. Believe that you can do it and you will. The only way to dispel the doubt that you can do something is to finish it.

Always be the best you can be. Never fall short from fatigue or lethargy. Don't attempt to do anything that you can't give your all to.

There is no way to inner satisfaction without appealing to the higher consciousness. Search within and without to find the paths that are meant for you and follow them with conviction and a steady heart.

And, you will succeed to become as rich and full as you ever desired.

Harold Ickes wanted the "freedom to live one's life with the window of the soul open to new thoughts, new ideas and new aspirations."

And Woody Allen looked for a clear path. "If only God would give me some clear sign" he said. "Like making a large deposit in my name at a Swiss bank."

Keys to Grow Rich

Focus

Focus is a scary word to most people. What can it do for us? How can it help us? Can we program ourselves to focus? Focus, confidence and self-discipline all work hand in hand with each other.

Learning to focus can help us in many ways. It can help us realise what we really want in life, it can help us make good and informed decisions. It can also help us to accept ourselves just the way we are, without feeling the need to condemn ourselves or put ourselves down in any way, shape or form.

Focus can help us gain confidence, power and happiness. Focus can also help us remain grounded and stay on track. Focus can change confusion into absolute knowledge and self-criticism into love for oneself.

Always be aware that you are able to focus on what you want, and to focus your thoughts on anything at all. Try it now by thinking about the dishes, now change your focus and think about your car. Switch focus again and think about a dog. It really is that easy to focus on whatever you want to focus on.

We all need to learn to set aside time to be used on the one thing we want or need to focus on. It's not a matter of "taking the time" to focus, but more a matter of "making the time". If we are willing to make the time, we will focus a lot better on whatever it is you want/need to do.

You ask me how I can possibly make time to focus with four demanding children, 3 dogs and a new house?

Easy, I can stay up for an extra hour when all the kids are in bed and the house is quiet, and MAKE the time to focus on what I'm doing with absolutely no distractions at all.

Oh, that's right; you work too, so you're too tired to stay up late. How about getting up half an hour early, before the madness at home begins? Before you go to bed, get everything ready for your early morning "focus time" so that you don't have to run around looking for it when you're half awake. Of course, this means you have to have a plan of action ready beforehand.

Decide when you are going to make time, and stick to it like glue. Don't let ANYTHING take you away from that time. Make sure you have everything you need all in one place, a room, or even a corner of a room where you can sit in peace. Unplug the phone, turn off the television, and don't even listen to quiet background music.

Whatever happens around you will distract you unless you learn how to focus. Sometimes it seems easier to just go along with these distractions than to focus on the end goal. Remember, if you let yourself go along with the distractions, you are losing sight of your goals. Sharpen your vision of what you want or you WILL be at the mercy of your environment.

When you want something you have to decide EXACTLY what it is you want. If you don't know what you want, there's no way on earth you're going to be able to focus on it. So you want to pass that driving test that you've taken and failed umpteen times, or you want to pass that really important exam in school.

You might want to write a book, or build a website, run your own business, be a teacher or any number of different things. The main thing is you have to KNOW that's what you want, and you have to set your aims high and demand yourself to focus on getting it.

Once you decide what you want, you have to decide WHY you want it. Visualize yourself in that brand new Mercedes or BMW, or in front of that school desk teaching the kids geography. The vision makes you feel good right? So that's why you want it, it feels good to do what you want to do, be who you want to be and own what you want to own.

Visualization is a major part in being able to focus. If you can actually see yourself in the position you want to be in, then it's so much easier to focus on the task of getting there.

Next thing you have to do is decide how you're going to actually get what you want. What are you willing to sacrifice in the quest to get those great exam grades? What can you do without in order to start up your own business? How can you make your family life happier and more peaceful?

Sit back and close your eyes, imagining what it will be like to have what you want in life, and think long and hard about what you can give up so that you can get there.

Say you want a new sofa, but the only way you can get one is if you quit smoking. Envision the sofa, with you and your partner cuddling up on it. What colour is it? Is it big and fluffed up, or is it a small ultra-modern sofa? Focus on the sofa and want it badly enough, you WILL stop smoking so you can get it.

These are all small things and perfectly attainable with a little bit of focus, but what if you want bigger and better things than that? Well then you set goals for yourself. First overcome the exams, once that goal is reached go get that driving licence. Next you get a brand spanking new BMW.

Keep setting goals; as soon as you reach the first one, move on to the next, staying focused all the time on what it is you want.

Reaching that first goal will give you an incredible boost of confidence, which in turn will make it so much easier to get started on the next goal. The more goals you reach, the more confidence you will have in yourself and that will fuel the success of the next goal, and the next one after that, until there are endless possibilities for you.

Start off by writing down each and every goal you WANT to reach in your lifetime. Then write a daily plan for the goal you want to reach first. Write the plan before you go to bed at night, it gives your brain time to take it all in and work with it.

It's amazing what the brain will do when we are sleeping. Also, writing the plan the night before helps free up that time during the next day so that you can purely sit and focus on the task at hand.

Make the plan a numbered list and cross each item off as you finish it. You'll be amazed at how quickly you get through it this way. Once you've reached the outcome you want, move on to your next goal following the same pattern as before.

If you find your thoughts wandering in your "focus time" take a break, write down your thoughts and put them away somewhere for future reference. If you find there are multiple things you can do to attain your goals, figure out which of them is the one most likely to help you get there quickest.

Put the others on hold, they may come in useful when you're aiming for that next goal.

If you lock your focus, and stick with it for as long as you have to, you WILL succeed. If you stick to one thing, one goal and focus on that, it's virtually impossible to not reap the rewards of your actions.

Confidence

Before we start, please keep one thing in mind; Confidence and arrogance are two totally different things. If you confuse the two, you will most certainly become a very unhappy person with very few real friends. Arrogance is NOT a "quality" and it won't help you reach your goals any faster.

Confidence in oneself, or the lack thereof is what stops people from getting tightly focused on what they want to achieve. That little voice telling them they can't do something is their biggest UN-motivator. What can YOU do to gain confidence?

25 tips toward boosting your confidence and self esteem.

1. Love Yourself:

This can take a bit of practice and looks really funny, but try it, it works. When you wake up, give yourself a great big hug. Do the same when it's time for sleep.

You've heard this said a million times before: "How can you expect others to love you if you don't love yourself?" It's true. Practice the morning and evening hugs for 2 weeks, maybe 3 weeks if you're the stubborn type, and you'll see how well it works.

2. Look in the mirror:

Every time you pass a mirror, look into it and flash your biggest and best smile at yourself. It might feel strange at first, but eventually it'll make you feel brilliant about yourself. Tell yourself "Looking good!" or "Wow, I love me!" or similar phrases often enough to actually start believing it.

3. Do things that make you feel good:

This can be anything from listening to music, trekking in the Andes, doing some volunteer work or even just taking a shower. Anything that gives you a positive feeling about yourself works for this one.

4. Listen to YOU:

Face it. Nobody knows you better than you know yourself, no matter how many people try to tell you differently. So if your body, mind or gut is telling you something, then take notice of it, and don't worry about what other people may possibly have to say about it.

5. Talk to YOU:

In times of stress, take a time-out break. Wander into your own mind and have a conversation with yourself about anything at all. Tell yourself how lucky you are to be you, and praise yourself for every good and positive thing you can attribute to yourself.

6. Remove negatives:

If anything feels like it's dragging you down, get rid of it. If it's clutter, tidy up, if it's a friend full of negativity explain nicely that you don't really feel up to talking right now. If it's your kids acting up, leave the room for a while and so on.

7. Surround with positives:

Surround yourself with things that bring out good feelings in you. Examples could be things such as happy, upbeat friends, a nice new picture, a new car, an old comfy blanket, candles, pictures of your family, your girlfriend, boyfriend, spouse etc.

8. Rumours Die:

Did you hear something about somebody who said something about somebody else? Drop it! Rumours are nasty, horrible things that will only bring you down. Best way to kill a rumour? Ignore it!

9. Total Honesty:

Be totally honest with yourself at all times. If there's something you don't like, admit it. If there's something you don't want to do "right now" and it isn't necessary for health and safety reasons then just don't do it until you feel like it.

Same goes for the positive aspects. If there's something you want to do, and it's not hurting anybody, then go ahead and do it. If you start feeling great about yourself for no apparent reason admit it and enjoy the feeling.

10. Responsibility

Take full responsibility for your own actions. Don't shove the blame for anything over onto someone or something else. We all make choices in our lives, and once we take responsibility for those choices we tend to choose better for ourselves.

Once we start to choose better, we feel better and things start falling into place. On the other hand, don't take over someone else's responsibilities just because you feel "you have to".

11. Pretend:

If you feel unsafe, unsure or nervous then go inside yourself and pretend you're a hot-shot lawyer, actor, actress, singer or whatever you need to be.

Make believe you're presenting yourself as that person would until you feel better. Trust me, you WILL feel better, and eventually have no need to be anything but yourself.

12. Keep Trying:

If you're trying to do something but don't get it right first time round, then try again, and again, and again, constantly learning from your mistakes until you get it right. When you finally DO get it right, you'll feel wonderful about it.

13. Credit where credit is due:

If you've done something really good, and people compliment you on it, accept the compliments with thanks! Understand that they're complimenting because they really ARE impressed with what you've done.

Believe in you and give yourself a pat on the back. (Although physically it would probably be easier to just give yourself a round of applause).

14. Stand Tall:

Standing up straight will ALWAYS make you feel better about yourself than slouching does. Stand with your feet slightly apart, suck in your tummy and behind, broaden your shoulders and straighten your neck. It's an amazingly quick confidence boost.

15. Say Hello:

Make it a rule to say hi to at least one person you don't know EVERY day. Give them the smile you flash at yourself in the mirror, the biggest and best one you can find. They'll smile back automatically, and they'll walk away with a little extra confidence boost thanks to you.

People look their best when they smile, and they also feel better by smiling too! This ultimately means you get a confidence boost too, for making someone else feel good about themselves.

16. Never Say Never....Ever:

If you think something can't be done, then you'll end up proving yourself right eventually. So never say never, just keep plugging along until it works for you.

If other people are telling you it can't be done, you're going to feel such immense satisfaction at actually doing it that your confidence will soar.

17. Get Active:

Don't sit around the house just doing nothing. Get up, go out, cycling, walking, exercising, anything that might invigorate your brain. A lively brain full of thoughts will help you gain confidence.

18. "Happy Foods":

Happy foods, such as chocolate, strawberries, lemons, ice-cream etc will increase the serotonin levels in your brain, leading to an increased feeling of happiness.

Feeling happy is a natural confidence boost. So go on, enjoy your food! (in moderation, of course).

19. Face Your Fear:

Is there something you are afraid of? Face it full on. Doing something scary and overcoming the fear is a fantastic way to boost your confidence. So go on, jump out of that plane (with a parachute of course), drive that car, speak in front of a large crowd, ask for a promotion, or whatever it is that scares you. You'll feel absolutely brilliant once it's done.

20. Willpower:

Create a goal that you really want to reach. Possibly something like weight loss before a certain time, giving up smoking or having a certain amount of money in the bank within so many months etc. Take baby steps, and use your willpower until you succeed at reaching your goal.

It will be really hard, as will power can be very elusive at times, but keep going and don't give up. Once you have reached that first goal by using your willpower you will have the confidence to create new goals AND reach them.

21. Ask questions:

Any time you find yourself worrying about something you haven't done, or something you think you should have done, ask yourself positive questions. Instead of thinking "I'm terrible for missing my friend's birthday" think "What can I do to make my friend feel special?"

Or, instead of "Why can't I ever seem to do things on time?" change it to "What can I change to better manage my time" Creating positive questions will release the negative energies which have a tendency to pull down your self confidence.

22. Learn:

Accept that not everything works out the way we plan it. Decide to accept any mistakes and rejections as part of a learning curve that we all need to go through.

Without mistakes, you can't learn from your own experiences. Remember, experience builds confidence, so always learn as much as you can.

23. List:

Write a list of every single thing you're good at, anything from clipping the dog's toenails to putting up a shelf. Take the time to sit and actually think about what you ARE good at and add them all to the list. You'll be surprised at how many things you end up jotting down, no matter how minor or trivial they may seem at the time.

Whenever you have a spare 5 minutes, or if you're feeling a little low, take the list out of your pocket and read it. This is a great little way to give yourself a nice confidence boost.

24: Help out:

There are lots of ways to help others, and feeling useful and helpful are great ways of building your confidence. Just make sure you do things because you WANT to do them. You could call a good friend who may be down at the moment-even take them out for coffee, you will brighten both your days, or you could possibly help out at an old folks home or similar. Knowing that people appreciate your help will boost your confidence for sure.

25: Show the way:

Think of the one thing you do best of all. Think long and hard about this one. Thought of something? Now, find a discussion group or similar related to that topic and spread your wisdom by answering questions, offering advice or help to anybody needing it. If you can't find a group, you could even start one yourself.

People will look up to you and that will give you all the more reason to feel confident about yourself.

Self-Discipline

To really be able to focus demands a lot of self-discipline. Remember that your outcome depends on YOU, not on the world around you. If you want something badly enough you WILL do everything in your power to get it.

Self-discipline in this context is basically only letting yourself do what you WANT to do at that precise moment in time to be able to reach your goals more quickly.

Remember that YOU are the boss of your actions. YOU are the one who is in control. So ultimately YOU decide what and when to do things you need to do to achieve your ultimate success.

Your ability to manage your actions is directly related to the level of success and happiness you will experience throughout your life. Managing your actions is commonly known as exercising self-discipline.

It's absolutely not about restricting your lifestyle, or punishing yourself. It's about being able to work with your thoughts, behaviour and actions in order to reach the goals that you wish to reach.

Not having self-discipline is one of the main reasons why we fail at what we want to do, both professionally and personally. Excuse-making often creates lack of self-discipline, so drop all your excuses and start keeping habits that in themselves will create the self-discipline you need. Make routines that you know you are capable of sticking to, and keep them.

How do you attain self-discipline? A few options could be regular exercise, better, healthier eating, even learning to spend less money. It could be something like deciding to learn something new every single day or just getting up an hour earlier than you normally would.

Having self-discipline will help you to complete the most boring and mundane of the tasks you are focusing on. Should you find yourself sitting and thinking thoughts like "Oh, I'll just do this instead" or "I can do that some other time" when you are working on your goals then STOP, take a deep breath and remember your self-discipline.

Golden Rules for Making Money

About Barnum:

Phineas Taylor Barnum (July 5, 1810 – April 7, 1891) was an American showman, businessman, scam artist and entertainer, remembered for promoting celebrated hoaxes and for founding the circus that became the Ringling Bros. and Barnum & Bailey Circus. Although Barnum was also an author, publisher, philanthropist, and for some time a politician, he said of himself, "I am a showman by profession... and all the gilding shall make nothing else of me," and his personal aims were "to put money in his own coffers." Barnum is widely but erroneously credited with coining the phrase "There's a sucker born every minute."

Barnum became a small-business owner in his early twenties, and founded a weekly newspaper, before moving to New York City in 1834. He embarked on an entertainment career, first with a variety troupe called "Barnum's Grand Scientific and

Musical Theater," and soon after by purchasing Scudder's American Museum, which he renamed after himself.

Barnum used the museum as a platform to promote hoaxes and human curiosities. The circus business was the source of much of his enduring fame. He established "P. T. Barnum's Grand Traveling Museum, Menagerie, Caravan & Hippodrome," a traveling circus, menagerie and museum of "freaks," which adopted many names over the years. Barnum wrote several books, including *Life of P.T. Barnum* (1854), *The Humbugs of the World* (1865), *Struggles and Triumphs* (1869), and *The Art of Money-Getting* (1880).

One of Barnum's more successful methods of self-promotion was mass publication of his autobiography.

Barnum eventually gave up his copyright to allow other printers to sell inexpensive editions. At the end of the 19th century the number of copies printed was second only to the New Testament in North America.

Don't Mistake Your Vocation

The safest plan, and the one most sure of success for the young man starting in life, is to select the vocation which is most congenial to his tastes. Parents and guardians are often quite too negligent in regard to this. It is very common for a father to say, for example: "I have five boys. I will make Billy a clergyman; John a lawyer; Tom a doctor, and Dick a farmer."

He then goes into town and looks about to see what he will do with Sammy. He returns home and says "Sammy, I see watchmaking is a nice, genteel business; I think I will make you a goldsmith." He does this, regardless of Sam's natural inclinations,or genius.

We are all, no doubt, born for a wise purpose. There is as much diversity in our brains as in our countenances. Some are born natural mechanics, while some have great aversion to machinery.

Let a dozen boys of ten years get together, and you will soon observe two or three are "whittling" out some ingenious device; working with locks or complicated machinery.

When they were but five years old, their father could find no toy to please them like a puzzle. They are natural mechanics;

but the other eight or nine boys have different aptitudes. I belong to the latter class; I never had the slightest love for mechanism; on the contrary, I have a sort of abhorrence for complicated machinery. I never had ingenuity enough to whittle a cider tap so it would not leak. I never could make a pen that I could write with, or understand the principle of a steam engine.

If a man was to take such a boy as I was, and attempt to make a watchmaker of him, the boy might, after an apprenticeship of five or seven years, be able to take apart and put together a watch; but all through life he would be working up hill and seizing every excuse for leaving his work and idling away his time. Watchmaking is repulsive to him.

Unless a man enters upon the vocation intended for him by nature, and best suited to his peculiar genius, he cannot succeed.

I am glad to believe that the majority of persons do find their right vocation. Yet we see many who have mistaken their calling, from the blacksmith up (or down) to the clergyman.

You will see, for instance, that extraordinary linguist the "learned blacksmith," who ought to have been a teacher of languages; and you may have seen lawyers, doctors and clergymen who were better fitted by nature for the anvil or the lapstone.

Select The Right Location

After securing the right vocation, you must be careful to select the proper location. You may have been cut out for a hotel keeper, and they say it requires a genius to "know how to keep a hotel." You might conduct a hotel like clock-work, and provide satisfactorily for five hundred guests every day; yet, if you should locate your house in a small village where there is no railroad communication or public travel, the location would be your ruin. It is equally important that you do not commence business where there are already enough to meet all demands in the same occupation. I remember a case which illustrates this subject.

When I was in London in 1858, I was passing down Holborn with an English friend and came to the "penny shows." They had immense cartoons outside, portraying the wonderful curiosities to be seen "all for a penny." Being a little in the "show line" myself, I said "let us go in here." We soon found ourselves in the presence of the illustrious showman, and he proved to be the sharpest man in that line I had ever met.

He told us some extraordinary stories in reference to his bearded ladies, his Albinos, and his Armadillos, which we could hardly believe, but thought it "better to believe it than look after the proof." He finally begged to call our attention to some wax statuary, and showed us a lot of the dirtiest and filthiest wax figures imaginable. They looked as if they had not seen water since the Deluge.

"What is there so wonderful about your statuary?" I asked.

"I beg you not to speak so satirically," he replied, "Sir, these are not Madam Tussaud's wax figures, all covered with gilt and tinsel and imitation diamonds, and copied from engravings and photographs. Mine, sir, were taken from life. Whenever you look upon one of those figures, you may consider that you are looking upon the living individual."

Glancing casually at them, I saw one labelled "Henry VIII," and feeling a little curious upon seeing that it looked like Calvin Edson, the living skeleton, I said: "Do you call that `Henry the Eighth?'" He replied, "Certainly, sir; it was taken from life at Hampton Court, by special order of his majesty, on such a day." He would have given the hour of the day if I had insisted; I said, "Everybody knows that `Henry VIII.' was a great stout old king, and that figure is lean and lank; what do you say to that?"

"Why," he replied, "you would be lean and lank yourself, if you sat there as long as he has."

There was no resisting such arguments. I said to my English

friend, "Let us go out; do not tell him who I am; I show the white feather; he beats me."

He followed us to the door, and seeing the rabble in the street, he called out, "ladies and gentlemen, I beg to draw your attention to the respectable character of my visitors," pointing to us as we walked away. I called upon him a couple of days afterwards; told him who I was, and said:

"My friend, you are an excellent showman, but you have selected a bad location."

He replied, "This is true, sir; I feel that all my talents are thrown away; but what can I do?"

"You can go to America," I replied. "You can give full play to your faculties over there; you will find plenty of elbow-room in America; I will engage you for two years; after that you will be ble to go on your own account."

He accepted my offer and remained two years in my New York Museum. He then went to New Orleans and carried on a traveling show business during the summer. To-day he is worth sixty thousand dollars, simply because he selected the right vocation and also secured the proper location. The old proverb says, "Three removes are as bad as a fire," but when a man is in the fire, it matters but little how soon or how often he removes.

Avoid Debt

Young men starting in life should avoid running into debt. There is scarcely anything that drags a person down like debt. It is a slavish position to get in, yet we find many a young man, hardly out of his "teens," running in debt. He meets a chum and says, "Look at this: I have got trusted for a new suit of clothes." He seems to look upon the clothes as so much given to him; well, it frequently is so, but, if he succeeds in paying and then gets trusted again, he is adopting a habit which will keep him in poverty through life. Debt robs a man of his self-respect, and makes him almost despise himself.

Grunting and groaning and working for what he has eaten up or worn out, and now when he is called upon to pay up, he has nothing to show for his money; this is properly termed "working for a dead horse." I do not speak of merchants buying and selling on credit, or of those who buy on credit in order to turn the purchase to a profit. The old Quaker said to his farmer son, "John, never get trusted; but if thee gets trusted for anything, let it be for `manure,' because that will help thee pay it back again."

Mr. Beecher advised young men to get in debt if they could to a small amount in the purchase of land, in the country districts.

"If a young man," he says, "will only get in debt for some land and then get married, these two things will keep him straight, or nothing will." This may be safe to a limited extent, but getting in debt for what you eat and drink and wear is to be avoided. Some families have a foolish habit of getting credit at "the stores," and thus frequently purchase many things which might have been dispensed with.

It is all very well to say, "I have got trusted for sixty days, and if I don't have the money the creditor will think nothing about it." There is no class of people in the world, who have such good memories as creditors. When the sixty days run out, you will have to pay. If you do not pay, you will break your promise, and probably resort to a falsehood. You may make some excuse or get in debt elsewhere to pay it, but that only involves you the deeper.

A good-looking, lazy young fellow, was the apprentice boy, Horatio. His employer said, "Horatio, did you ever see a snail?"

"I—think—I—have," he drawled out. "You must have met him then, for I am sure you never overtook one," said the "boss."

Your creditor will meet you or overtake you and say, "Now, my young friend, you agreed to pay me; you have not done it, you must give me your note." You give the note on interest and it commences working against you; "it is a dead horse." The creditor goes to bed at night and wakes up in the morning better off than when he retired to bed, because his interest has increased during the night, but you grow poorer while you are sleeping, for the interest is accumulating against you.

Money is in some respects like fire; it is a very excellent servant but a terrible master. When you have it mastering you; when interest is constantly piling up against you, it will keep you down in the worst kind of slavery. But let money work for you, and you have the most devoted servant in the world. It is no "eye-servant." There is nothing animate or inanimate that will work so faithfully as money when placed at interest, well secured. It works night and day, and in wet or dry weather.

I was born in the blue-law State of Connecticut, where the old Puritans had laws so rigid that it was said, "they fined a man for kissing his wife on Sunday." Yet these rich old Puritans would have thousands of dollars at interest, and on Saturday night would be worth a certain amount; on Sunday they would go to church and perform all the duties of a Christian. On waking up on Monday morning, they would find themselves considerably richer than the Saturday night previous, simply because their money placed at interest had worked faithfully for them all day Sunday, according to law!

Do not let it work against you; if you do there is no chance for success in life so far as money is concerned. John Randolph, the eccentric Virginian, once exclaimed in Congress, "Mr. Speaker, I have discovered the philosopher's stone: pay as you go." This is, indeed, nearer to the philosopher's stone than any alchemist has ever yet arrived.

Persevere

When a man is in the right path, he must persevere. I speak of this because there are some persons who are "born tired;" naturally lazy and possessing no self-reliance and no perseverance.

But they can cultivate these qualities, as Davy Crockett said:

"This thing remember, when I am dead, Be sure you are right, then go ahead." It is this go-aheaditiveness, this determination not to let the "horrors" or the "blues" take possession of you, so as to make you relax your energies in the struggle for independence, which you must cultivate.

How many have almost reached the goal of their ambition, but, losing faith in themselves, have relaxed their energies, and the golden prize has been lost forever. It is, no doubt, often true, as Shakespeare says:

"There is a tide in the affairs of men, which taken at the flood, leads on to fortune."

If you hesitate, some bolder hand will stretch out before you and get the prize. Remember the proverb of Solomon: "He becometh poor that dealeth with a slack hand; but the hand of the diligent maketh rich."

Perseverance is sometimes but another word for self-reliance.

Many persons naturally look on the dark side of life, and borrow trouble. They are born so. Then they ask for advice, and they will be governed by one wind and blown by another, and cannot rely upon themselves. Until you can get so that you can rely upon yourself, you need not expect to succeed. I have known men, personally, who have met with pecuniary reverses, and absolutely committed suicide, because they thought they could never overcome their misfortune. But I have known others who have met more serious financial difficulties, and have bridged them over by simple perseverance, aided by a firm belief that they were doing justly, and that Providence would "overcome evil with good." You will see this illustrated in any sphere of life.

Take two generals; both understand military tactics, both educated at West Point, if you please, both equally gifted; yet one, having this principle of perseverance, and the other lacking it, the former will succeed in his profession, while the latter will fail. One may hear the cry, "the enemy are coming, and they have got cannon."

"Got cannon?" says the hesitating general.

"Yes."

"Then halt every man."

He wants time to reflect; his hesitation is his ruin; the enemy passes unmolested, or overwhelms him; while on the other hand, the general of pluck, perseverance and self-reliance, goes into battle with a will, and, amid the clash of arms, the booming of cannon, the shrieks of the wounded, and the moans of the dying, you will see this man persevering, going on, cutting and slashing his way through with unwavering determination, inspiring his soldiers to deeds of fortitude, valor, and triumph.

Whatever You Do, Do It With All Your Might

Work at it, if necessary, early and late, in season and out of season, not leaving a stone unturned, and never deferring for a single hour that which can be done just as well *now*. The old proverb is full of truth and meaning, "Whatever is worth doing at all, is worth doing well." Many a man acquires a fortune by doing his business thoroughly, while his neighbor remains poor for life, because he only half does it. Ambition, energy, industry, perseverance, are indispensable requisites for success in business.

Fortune always favors the brave, and never helps a man who does not help himself. It won't do to spend your time like Mr. Micawber, in waiting for something to "turn up." To such men one of two things usually "turns up:" the poor-house or the jail; for idleness breeds bad habits, and clothes a man in rags. The poor spendthrift vagabond says to a rich man:

"I have discovered there is enough money in the world for all of us, if it was equally divided; this must be done, and we shall all be happy together."

"But," was the response, "if everybody was like you, it would be spent in two months, and what would you do then?"

"Oh! divide again; keep dividing, of course!"

I was recently reading in a London paper an account of a like philosophic pauper who was kicked out of a cheap boardinghouse because he could not pay his bill, but he had a roll of papers sticking out of his coat pocket, which, upon examination, proved to be his plan for paying off the national debt of England without the aid of a penny.

People have got to do as Cromwell said: "not only trust in Providence, but keep the powder dry." Do your part of the work, or you cannot succeed. Mahomet, one night, while encamping in the desert, overheard one of his fatigued followers remark: "I will loose my camel, and trust it to God!" "No, no, not so," said the prophet, "tie thy camel, and trust it to God!" Do all you can for yourselves, and then trust to Providence, or luck, or whatever you please to call it, for the rest.

Depend Upon Your Own Personal Exertions

The eye of the employer is often worth more than the hands of a dozen employees. In the nature of things, an agent cannot be so faithful to his employer as to himself. Many who are employers will call to mind instances where the best employees have overlooked important points which could not have escaped their own observation as a proprietor.

No man has a right to expect to succeed in life unless he understands his business, and nobody can understand his business thoroughly unless he learns it by personal application and experience.

A man may be a manufacturer; he has got to learn the many details of his business personally; he will learn something every day, and he will find he will make mistakes nearly every day. And these very mistakes are helps to him in the way of experiences if he but heeds them. He will be like the Yankee tin-peddler, who, having been cheated as to quality in the purchase of his merchandise, said: "All right, there's a little information to be gained every day; I will never be cheated in that way again."

Thus a man buys his experience, and it is the best kind if not purchased at too dear a rate.

I hold that every man should, like Cuvier, the French naturalist, thoroughly know his business. So proficient was he in the study of natural history, that you might bring to him the bone, or even a section of a bone of an animal which he had never seen described, and, reasoning from analogy, he would be able to draw a picture of the object from which the bone had been taken. On one occasion his students attempted to deceive him.

They rolled one of their number in a cow skin and put him under the professor's table as a new specimen. When the philosopher came into the room, some of the students asked him what animal it was. Suddenly the animal said "I am the devil and I am going to eat you." It was but natural that Cuvier should desire to classify this creature, and examining it intently, he said:

"Divided hoof; graminivorous! it cannot be done."

He knew that an animal with a split hoof must live upon grass and grain, or other kind of vegetation, and would not be inclined to eat flesh, dead or alive, so he considered himself perfectly safe. The possession of a perfect knowledge of your business is an absolute necessity in order to insure success.

Among the maxims of the elder Rothschild was one, an apparent paradox: "Be cautions and bold." This seems to he a contradiction in terms, but it is not, and there is great wisdom in the maxim. It is, in fact, a condensed statement of what I have already said. It is to say, "you must exercise your caution in laying your plans, but be bold in carrying them out." A man who is all caution, will never dare to take hold and be successful; and a man who is all boldness, is merely reckless, and must eventually fail. A man may go on "'change" and make fifty or one hundred thousand dollars in speculating in stocks, at a single operation. But if he has simple boldness without caution, it is mere chance, and what he gains to-day he will lose to-morrow.

You must have both the caution and the boldness, to insure success.

The Rothschilds have another maxim: "Never have anything to do with an unlucky man or place." That is to say, never have anything to do with a man or place which never succeeds, because, although a man may appear to be honest and intelligent, yet if he tries this or that thing and always fails, it is on account of some fault or infirmity that you may not be able to discover but nevertheless which must exist.

There is no such thing in the world as luck. There never was a man who could go out in the morning and find a purse full of gold in the street to-day, and another to-morrow, and so on, day after day. He may do so once in his life; but so far as mere luck is concerned, he is as liable to lose it as to find it. "Like causes produce like effects." If a man adopts the proper methods to be successful, "luck" will not prevent him. If he does not succeed, there are reasons for it, although, perhaps, he may not be able to see them.

Don't Get Above Your Business

Young men after they get through their business training, or apprenticeship, instead of pursuing their avocation and rising in their business, will often lie about doing nothing. They say, "I have learned my business, but I am not going to be a hireling; what is the object of learning my trade or profession, unless I establish myself?"

"Have you capital to start with?"

"No, but I am going to have it."

"How are you going to get it?"

"I will tell you confidentially; I have a wealthy old aunt, and she will die pretty soon; but if she does not, I expect to find some rich old man who will lend me a few thousands to give

me a start. If I only get the money to start with I will do well."

There is no greater mistake than when a young man believes he will succeed with borrowed money. Why? Because every man's experience coincides with that of Mr. Astor, who said, "it was more difficult for him to accumulate his first thousand dollars, than all the succeeding millions that made up his colossal fortune."

Money is good for nothing unless you know the value of it by experience. Give a boy twenty thousand dollars and put him in business, and the chances are that he will lose every dollar of it before he is a year older. Like buying a ticket in the lottery, and drawing a prize, it is "easy come, easy go." He does not know the value of it; nothing is worth anything, unless it costs effort.

Without self-denial and economy, patience and perseverance, and commencing with capital which you have not earned, you are not sure to succeed in accumulating.

Young men, instead of "waiting for dead men's shoes," should be up and doing, for there is no class of persons who are so unaccommodating in regard to dying as these rich old people, and it is fortunate for the expectant heirs that it is so. Nine out of ten of the rich men of our country to-day, started out in life as poor boys, with determined wills, industry, perseverance, economy and good habits.

They went on gradually, made their own money and saved it; and this is the best way to acquire a fortune. Stephen Girard started life as a poor cabin boy, and died worth nine million dollars. A. T. Stewart was a poor Irish boy; and he paid taxes on a million and a half dollars of income, per year.

John Jacob Astor was a poor farmer boy, and died worth twenty millions. Cornelius Vanderbilt began life rowing a boat from Staten Island to New York; he presented our government with a steamship worth a million of dollars, and died worth fifty millions.

"There is no royal road to learning," says the proverb, and I may say it is equally true, "there is no royal road to wealth." But I think there is a royal road to both. The road to learning is a royal one; the road that enables the student to expand his intellect and add every day to his stock of knowledge, until, in the pleasant process of intellectual growth, he is able to solve the most profound problems, to count the stars, to analyze every atom of the globe, and to measure the firmament—this is a regal highway, and it is the only road worth traveling.

So in regard to wealth. Go on in confidence, study the rules, and above all things, study human nature; for "the proper study of mankind is man," and you will find that while expanding the intellect and the muscles, your enlarged experience will enable you every day to accumulate more and more principal, which will increase itself by interest and otherwise, until you arrive at a state of independence. You will find, as a general thing, that the poor boys get rich and the rich boys get poor.

For instance, a rich man at his decease, leaves a large estate to his family. His eldest sons, who have helped him earn his fortune, know by experience the value of money, and they take their inheritance and add to it. The separate portions of the young children are placed at interest, and the little fellows are patted on the head, and told a dozen times a day, "you are rich; you will never have to work, you can always have whatever you wish, for you were born with a golden spoon in your mouth."

The young heir soon finds out what that means; he has the finest dresses and playthings; he is crammed with sugar candies and almost "killed with kindness," and he passes from school to school, petted and flattered. He becomes arrogant and self-conceited, abuses his teachers, and carries everything with a high hand. He knows nothing of the real value of money, having never earned any; but he knows all about the "golden spoon" business.

At college, he invites his poor fellow-students to his room, where he "wines and dines" them. He is cajoled and caressed, and called a glorious good fellow, because he is so lavish of his money. He gives his game suppers, drives his fast horses, invites his chums to fetes and parties, determined to have lots of "good times." He spends the night in frolics and debauchery, and leads off his companions with the familiar song, "we won't go home till morning."

He gets them to join him in pulling down signs, taking gates from their hinges and throwing them into back yards and horse-ponds. If the police arrest them, he knocks them down, is taken to the lock-up, and joyfully foots the bills.

"Ah! my boys," he cries, "what is the use of being rich, if you can't enjoy yourself?"

He might more truly say, "if you can't make a fool of yourself;" but he is "fast," hates slow things, and don't "see it."

Young men loaded down with other people's money are almost sure to lose all they inherit, and they acquire all sorts of bad habits which, in the majority of cases, ruin them in health, purse and character. In this country, one generation follows another, and the poor of to-day are rich in the next generation, or the third.

Their experience leads them on, and they become rich, and they leave vast riches to their young children. These children, having been reared in luxury, are inexperienced and get poor; and after long experience another generation comes on and gathers up riches again in turn. And thus "history repeats itself," and happy is he who by listening to the experience of others avoids the rocks and shoals on which so many have been wrecked.

"In England, the business makes the man." If a man in that country is a mechanic or working-man, he is not recognized as a gentleman. On the occasion of my first appearance before Queen Victoria, the Duke of Wellington asked me what sphere in life General Tom Thumb's parents were in.

"His father is a carpenter," I replied.

"Oh! I had heard he was a gentleman," was the response of His Grace.

In this Republican country, the man makes the business. No matter whether he is a blacksmith, a shoemaker, a farmer, banker or lawyer, so long as his business is legitimate, he may be a gentleman. So any "legitimate" business is a double blessing— it helps the man engaged in it, and also helps others. The farmer supports his own family, but he also benefits the merchant or mechanic who needs the products of his farm.

The tailor not only makes a living by his trade, but he also benefits the farmer, the clergyman and others who cannot make their own clothing. But all these classes of men may be gentlemen.

The great ambition should be to *excel* all others engaged in the same occupation.

The college-student who was about graduating, said to an old lawyer:

"I have not yet decided which profession I will follow. Is your profession full?"

"The basement is much crowded, but there is plenty of room *up-stairs*," was the witty and truthful reply.

No profession, trade, or calling, is overcrowded in the upper story. Wherever you find the most honest and intelligent merchant or banker, or the best lawyer, the best doctor, the best clergyman, the best shoemaker, carpenter, or anything else, that man is most sought for, and has always enough to do. As a nation Americans are too superficial—they are striving to get rich quickly, and do not generally do their business as substantially and thoroughly as they should, but whoever *excels* all others in his own line, if his habits are good and his integrity undoubted, cannot fail to secure abundant patronage, and the wealth that naturally follows. Let your motto then always be "Excelsior," for by living up to it there is no such word as fail.

Every man should make his son or daughter learn some trade or profession, so that in these days of changing fortunes—of being rich to-day and poor to-morrow—they may have something tangible to fall back upon. This provision might save many persons from misery, who by some unexpected turn of fortune have lost all their means.

Many persons are always kept poor, because they are too visionary. Every project looks to them like certain success, and therefore they keep changing from one business to another, always in hot water, always "under the harrow." The plan of "counting the chickens before they are hatched" is an error of ancient date, but it does not seem to improve by age.

Do Not Scatter Your Powers

Engage in one kind of business only, and stick to it faithfully until you succeed, or until your experience shows that you should abandon it. A constant hammering on one nail will generally drive it home at last, so that it can be clinched. When a man's undivided attention is centered on one object, his mind will constantly be suggesting improvements of value, which would escape him if his brain was occupied by a dozen different subjects at once. Many a fortune has slipped through a man's fingers because he was engaged in too many occupations at a time. There is good sense in the old caution against having too many irons in the fire at

Be Systematic

Men should be systematic in their business. A person who does business by rule, having a time and place for everything, doing his work promptly, will accomplish twice as much and with half the trouble of him who does it carelessly and slipshod.

By introducing system into all your transactions, doing one thing at a time, always meeting appointments with punctuality, you find leisure for pastime and recreation; whereas the man who only half does one thing, and then turns to something else, and half does that, will have his business at loose ends, and will never know when his day's work is done, for it never will be done.

Of course, there is a limit to all these rules. We must try to preserve the happy medium, for there is such a thing as being too systematic. There are men and women, for instance, who put away things so carefully that they can never find them again. It is too much like the "red tape" formality at Washington, and Mr. Dickens' "Circumlocution Office,"—all theory and no result.

When the "Astor House" was first started in New York city, it was undoubtedly the best hotel in the country. The proprietors had learned a good deal in Europe regarding hotels, and the landlords were proud of the rigid system which pervaded every department of their great establishment. When twelve o'clock at night had arrived, and there were a number of guests around, one of the proprietors would say, "Touch that bell, John;" and in two minutes sixty servants, with a water-bucket in each hand, would present themselves in the hall. "This," said the landlord, addressing his guests, "is our fire-bell; it will show you we are quite safe here; we do everything systematically."

This was before the Croton water was introduced into the city. But they sometimes carried their system too far. On one occasion, when the hotel was thronged with guests, one of the waiters was suddenly indisposed, and although there were fifty waiters in the hotel, the landlord thought he must have his full complement, or his "system" would be interfered with. Just before dinner-time, he rushed down stairs and said, "There must be another waiter, I am one waiter short, what can I do?"

He happened to see "Boots," the Irishman. "Pat," said he, "wash your hands and face; take that white apron and come into the dining-room in five minutes." Presently Pat appeared as required, and the proprietor said: "Now Pat, you must stand behind these two chairs, and wait on the gentlemen who will occupy them; did you ever act as a waiter?"

"I know all about it, sure, but I never did it."

Like the Irish pilot, on one occasion when the captain, thinking he was considerably out of his course, asked, "Are you certain you understand what you are doing?"

Pat replied, "Sure and I knows every rock in the channel."

That moment, "bang" thumped the vessel against a rock.

"Ah! be jabers, and that is one of 'em," continued the pilot.

But to return to the dining-room, "Pat," said the landlord, "here we do everything systematically. You must first give the gentlemen each a plate of soup, and when they finish that, ask them what they will have next."

Pat replied, "Ah! an' I understand parfectly the vartues of shystem."

Very soon in came the guests. The plates of soup were placed before them. One of Pat's two gentlemen ate his soup; the other did not care for it. He said: "Waiter, take this plate away and bring me some fish." Pat looked at the untasted plate of soup, and remembering the injunctions of the landlord in regard to "system," replied: "Not till ye have ate yer supe!"

Of course that was carrying "system" entirely too far.

Always take a trustworthy newspaper, and thus keep thoroughly posted in regard to the transactions of the world. He who is without a newspaper is cut off from his species. In these days of telegraphs and steam, many important inventions and improvements in every branch of trade, are being made, and he who don't consult the newspapers will soon find himself and his business left out in the cold.

Beware Of "Outside Operations"

We sometimes see men who have obtained fortunes, suddenly become poor. In many cases, this arises from intemperance, and often from gaming, and other bad habits. Frequently it occurs because a man has been engaged in "outside operations," of some sort. When he gets rich in his legitimate business, he is told of a grand speculation where he can make a score of thousands.

He is constantly flattered by his friends, who tell him that he is born lucky, that everything he touches turns into gold. Now if he forgets that his economical habits, his rectitude of conduct and a personal attention to a business which he understood, caused his success in life, he will listen to the siren voices. He says:

"I will put in twenty thousand dollars. I have been lucky, and my good luck will soon bring me back sixty thousand dollars."

A few days elapse and it is discovered he must put in ten thousand dollars more; soon after he is told "it is all right," but certain matters not foreseen, require an advance of twenty thousand dollars more, which will bring him a rich harvest;

but before the time comes around to realize, the bubble bursts, he loses all he is possessed of, and then he learns what he ought to have known at the first, that however successful a man may be in his own business, if he turns from that and engages in a business which he don't understand, he is like Samson when shorn of his locks—his strength has departed, and he becomes like other men.

If a man has plenty of money, he ought to invest something in everything that appears to promise success, and that will probably benefit mankind; but let the sums thus invested be moderate in amount, and never let a man foolishly jeopardize a fortune that he has earned in a legitimate way, by investing it in things in which he has had no experience.

Don't Indorse Without Security

I hold that no man ought ever to indorse a note or become security for any man, be it his father or brother, to a greater extent than he can afford to lose and care nothing about, without taking good security. Here is a man that is worth twenty thousand dollars; he is doing a thriving manufacturing or mercantile trade; you are retired and living on your money; he comes to you and says:

"You are aware that I am worth twenty thousand dollars, and don't owe a dollar; if I had five thousand dollars in cash, I could purchase a particular lot of goods and double my money in a couple of months; will you indorse my note for that amount?"

You reflect that he is worth twenty thousand dollars, and you incur no risk by indorsing his note; you like to accommodate him, and you lend your name without taking the precaution of getting security. Shortly after, he shows you the note with your indorsement canceled, and tells you, probably truly, "that he made the profit that he expected by the operation," you reflect that you have done a good action, and the thought makes you feel happy. By and by, the same thing occurs again and you do it again; you have already fixed the impression in your mind that it is perfectly safe to indorse his notes without security.

But the trouble is, this man is getting money too easily. He has only to take your note to the bank, get it discounted and take the cash. He gets money for the time being without effort; without inconvenience to himself. Now mark the result. He sees a chance for speculation outside of his business. A temporary investment of only $10,000 is required. It is sure to come back before a note at the bank would be due. He places a note for that amount before you. You sign it almost mechanically. Being firmly convinced that your friend is responsible and trustworthy, you indorse his notes as a "matter of course."

Unfortunately the speculation does not come to a head quite so soon as was expected, and another $10,000 note must be discounted to take up the last one when due. Before this note matures the speculation has proved an utter failure and all the money is lost. Does the loser tell his friend, the indorser, that he has lost half of his fortune? Not at all. He don't even mention that he has speculated at all. But he has got excited; the spirit of speculation has seized him; he sees others making large sums in this way (we seldom hear of the losers), and, like other speculators, he "looks for his money where he loses it." He tries again. Indorsing notes has become chronic with you, and at every loss he gets your signature for whatever amount he wants.

Finally you discover your friend has lost all of his property and all of yours. You are overwhelmed with astonishment and grief, and you say "it is a hard thing; my friend here has ruined me," but, you should add, "I have also ruined him."

If you had said in the first place, "I will accommodate you, but I never indorse without taking ample security," he could not have gone beyond the length of his tether, and he would never have been tempted away from his legitimate business. It is a very dangerous thing, therefore, at any time, to let people get possession of money too easily; it tempts them to hazardous speculations, if nothing more. Solomon truly said "he that hateth suretiship is sure."

So with the young man starting in business; let him understand the value of money by earning it. When he does understand its value, then grease the wheels a little in helping him to start business, but remember, men who get money with too great facility, cannot usually succeed. You must get the first dollars by hard knocks, and at some sacrifice, in order to appreciate the value of those dollars.

Advertise Your Business

We all depend, more or less, upon the public for our support.

We all trade with the public—lawyers, doctors, shoemakers, artists, blacksmiths, showmen, opera singers, railroad presidents, and college professors. Those who deal with the public must be careful that their goods are valuable; that they are genuine, and will give satisfaction. When you get an article which you know is going to please your customers, and that when they have tried it, they will feel they have got their money's worth, then let the fact be known that you have got it.

Be careful to advertise it in some shape or other, because it is evident that if a man has ever so good an article for sale, and nobody knows it, it will bring him no return. In a country like this, where nearly everybody reads, and where newspapers are issued and circulated in editions of five thousand to two hundred thousand, it would be very unwise if this channel was not taken advantage of to reach the public in advertising.

A newspaper goes into the family, and is read by wife and children, as well as the head of the home; hence hundreds and thousands of people may read your advertisement, while you are attending to your routine business. Many, perhaps, read it while you are asleep.

The whole philosophy of life is, first "sow," then "reap." That is the way the farmer does; he plants his potatoes and corn, and sows his grain, and then goes about something else, and the time comes when he reaps. But he never reaps first and sows afterwards.

This principle applies to all kinds of business, and to nothing more eminently than to advertising. If a man has a genuine article, there is no way in which he can reap more advantageously than by "sowing" to the public in this way. He must, of course, have a really good article, and one which will please his customers; anything spurious will not succeed permanently because the public is wiser than many imagine. Men and women are selfish, and we all prefer purchasing where we can get the most for our money and we try to find out where we can most surely do so.

You may advertise a spurious article, and induce many people to call and buy it once, but they will denounce you as an imposter and swindler, and your business will gradually die out and leave you poor. This is right. Few people can safely depend upon chance custom. You all need to have your customers return and purchase again. A man said to me, "I have tried advertising and did not succeed; yet I have a good article."

I replied, "My friend, there may be exceptions to a general rule. But how do you advertise?"

"I put it in a weekly newspaper three times, and paid a dollar and a half for it."

I replied: "Sir, advertising is like learning—`a little is a dangerous thing!'"

A French writer says that "The reader of a newspaper does not see the first mention of an ordinary advertisement; the second insertion he sees, but does not read; the third insertion he reads; the fourth insertion, he looks at the price; the fifth insertion, he speaks of it to his wife; the sixth insertion, he is ready to purchase, and the seventh insertion, he purchases."

Your object in advertising is to make the public understand what you have got to sell, and if you have not the pluck to keep advertising, until you have imparted that information, all the money you have spent is lost.

You are like the fellow who told the gentleman if he would give him ten cents it would save him a dollar. "How can I help you so much with so small a sum?" asked the gentleman in surprise. "I started out this morning (hiccupped the fellow) with the full determination to get drunk, and I have spent my only dollar to accomplish the object, and it has not quite done it. Ten cents worth more of whiskey would just do it, and in this manner I should save the dollar already expended."

So a man who advertises at all must keep it up until the public know who and what he is, and what his business is, or else the money invested in advertising is lost.

Some men have a peculiar genius for writing a striking advertisement, one that will arrest the attention of the reader at first sight. This fact, of course, gives the advertiser a great advantage.

Sometimes a man makes himself popular by an unique sign or a curious display in his window. Recently I observed a swing sign extending over the sidewalk in front of a store, on which was the inscription in plain letters,"DON'T READ THE OTHER SIDE."

Of course I did, and so did everybody else, and I learned that the man had made an independence by first attracting the public to his business in that way and then using his customers well afterwards.

Genin, the hatter, bought the first Jenny Lind ticket at auction for two hundred and twenty-five dollars, because he knew it would be a good advertisement for him. "Who is the bidder?" said the auctioneer, as he knocked down that ticket at Castle Garden. "Genin, the hatter," was the response. Here were thousands of people from the Fifth avenue, and from distant cities in the highest stations in life. "Who is `Genin,' the hatter?" they exclaimed. They had never heard of him before.

The next morning the newspapers and telegraph had circulated the facts from Maine to Texas, and from five to ten millions of people had read that the tickets sold at auction for Jenny Lind's first concert amounted to about twenty thousand dollars, and that a single ticket was sold at two hundred and twenty-five dollars, to "Genin, the hatter."

Men throughout the country involuntarily took off their hats to see if they had a "Genin" hat on their heads. At a town in Iowa it was found that in the crowd around the post office, there was one man who had a "Genin" hat, and he showed it in triumph, although it was worn out and not worth two cents. "Why," one man exclaimed, "you have a real `Genin' hat; what a lucky fellow you are."

Another man said, "Hang on to that hat, it will be a valuable heir-loom in your family." Still another man in the crowd who seemed to envy the possessor of this good fortune, said, "Come, give us all a chance; put it up at auction!" He did so, and it was sold as a keepsake for nine dollars and fifty cents! What was the consequence to Mr. Genin? He sold ten thousand extra hats per annum, the first six years. Nine-tenths of the purchasers bought of him, probably, out of curiosity, and many of them, finding that he gave them an equivalent for their money, became his regular customers. This novel advertisement first struck their attention, and then, as he made a good article, they came again.

Now I don't say that everybody should advertise as Mr. Genin did. But I say if a man has got goods for sale, and he don't advertise them in some way, the chances are that some day the sheriff will do it for him. Nor do I say that everybody must advertise in a newspaper, or indeed use "printers' ink" at all. On the contrary, although that article is indispensable in the majority of cases, yet doctors and clergymen, and sometimes lawyers and some others, can more effectually reach the public in some other manner. But it is obvious, they must be known in some way, else how could they be supported?

Be Polite And Kind To Your Customers

Politeness and civility are the best capital ever invested in business. Large stores, gilt signs, flaming advertisements, will all prove unavailing if you or your employees treat your patrons abruptly. The truth is, the more kind and liberal a man is, the more generous will be the patronage bestowed upon him.

"Like begets like." The man who gives the greatest amount of goods of a corresponding quality for the least sum (still reserving for himself a profit) will generally succeed best in the long run. This brings us to the golden rule, "As ye would that men should do to you, do ye also to them," and they will do better by you than if you always treated them as if you wanted to get the most you could out of them for the least return.

Men who drive sharp bargains with their customers, acting as if they never expected to see them again, will not be mistaken.

They will never see them again as customers. People don't like to pay and get kicked also.

One of the ushers in my Museum once told me he intended to whip a man who was in the lecture-room as soon as he came out.

"What for?" I inquired.

"Because he said I was no gentleman," replied the usher.

"Never mind," I replied, "he pays for that, and you will not convince him you are a gentleman by whipping him. I cannot afford to lose a customer. If you whip him, he will never visit the Museum again, and he will induce friends to go with him to other places of amusement instead of this, and thus you see, I should be a serious loser."

"But he insulted me," muttered the usher.

"Exactly," I replied, "and if he owned the Museum, and you had paid him for the privilege of visiting it, and he had then insulted you, there might be some reason in your resenting it, but in this instance he is the man who pays, while we receive, and you must, therefore, put up with his bad manners."

My usher laughingly remarked, that this was undoubtedly the true policy, but he added that he should not object to an increase of salary if he was expected to be abused in order to promote my interest.

Don't Blab

Some men have a foolish habit of telling their business secrets. If they make money they like to tell their neighbors how it was done. Nothing is gained by this, and ofttimes much is lost. Say nothing about your profits, your hopes, your expectations, your intentions. And this should apply to letters as well as to conversation.

Goethe makes Mephistophiles say: "Never write a letter nor destroy one." Business men must write letters, but they should be careful what they put in them. If you are losing money, be specially cautious and not tell of it, or you will lose your reputation.

Preserve Your Integrity

It is more precious than diamonds or rubies. The old miser said to his sons: "Get money; get it honestly, if you can, but get money."

This advice was not only atrociously wicked, but it was the very essence of stupidity. It was as much as to say, "if you find it difficult to obtain money honestly, you can easily get it dishonestly. Get it in that way." Poor fool! Not to know that the most difficult thing in life is to make money dishonestly! not to know that our prisons are full of men who attempted to follow this advice; not to understand that no man can be dishonest, without soon being found out, and that when his lack of principle is discovered, nearly every avenue to success is closed against him forever.

The public very properly shun all whose integrity is doubted. No matter how polite and pleasant and accommodating a man may be, none of us dare to deal with him if we suspect "false weights and measures." Strict honesty, not only lies at the foundation of all success in life (financially), but in every other respect.

Uncompromising integrity of character is invaluable. It secures to its possessor a peace and joy which cannot be attained without it—which no amount of money, or houses and lands can purchase. A man who is known to be strictly honest, may be ever so poor, but he has the purses of all the community at his disposal—for all know that if he promises to return what he borrows, he will never disappoint them.

As a mere matter of selfishness, therefore, if a man had no higher motive for being honest, all will find that the maxim of Dr. Franklin can never fail to be true, that "honesty is the best policy."

To get rich, is not always equivalent to being successful. "There are many rich poor men," while there are many others, honest and devout men and women, who have never possessed so much money as some rich persons squander in a week, but who are nevertheless really richer and happier than any man can ever be while he is a transgressor of the higher laws of his being.

The inordinate love of money, no doubt, may be and is "the root of all evil," but money itself, when properly used, is not only a "handy thing to have in the house," but affords the gratification of blessing our race by enabling its possessor to enlarge the scope of human happiness and human influence.

The desire for wealth is nearly universal, and none can say it is not laudable, provided the possessor of it accepts its responsibilities, and uses it as a friend to humanity.

The history of money-getting, which is commerce, is a history of civilization, and wherever trade has flourished most, there, too, have art and science produced the noblest fruits. In fact, as a general thing, money-getters are the benefactors of our race. To them, in a great measure, are we indebted for our institutions of learning and of art, our academies, colleges and churches. It is no argument against the desire for, or the possession of, wealth, to say that there are sometimes misers who hoard money only for the sake of hoarding and who have no higher aspiration than to grasp everything which comes within their reach.

As we have sometimes hypocrites in religion, and demagogues in politics, so there are occasionally misers among money-getters. These, however, are only exceptions to the general rule. But when, in this country, we find such a nuisance and stumbling block as a miser, we remember with gratitude that in America we have no laws of primogeniture, and that in the due course of nature the time will come when the hoarded dust will be scattered for the benefit of mankind.

To all men and women, therefore, do I conscientiously say, make money honestly, and not otherwise, for Shakespeare has truly said, "He that wants money, means, and content, is without three good friends."

Internet marketing a big advantage to many businesses

Internet marketing is now called so many other names – e-marketing, web marketing, i-marketing, digital marketing, online marketing and the like. However, in plain and simple language, it can be defined as the marketing of one's products or services that a business or person offers through the use of the internet.

This type of marketing encompasses a very broad area of the subject as it also includes many types of marketing strategies like e-mail and wireless media marketing. Under this general scope of internet marketing also falls the aspects of ECRM or electronic customer relationship management and digital customer data.

The world wide web has given us many unique and essential benefits. This technology enabled the entire world to be connected with each other in a matter of seconds. In terms of online businesses, the internet has provided a global portal in which goods and services can be sold and bought by almost anyone and in any part of the world.

With internet marketing, all types of businesses have enjoyed the lower costs of information dissemination and advertisements. The internet's interactive nature has benefited business marketing through instant responses and its ability to elicit them in the fastest way possible. Furthermore, internet marketing has tied together all the aspects of creativity, technicality, advertisement, sales and product development.

With its inexpensive cost, internet marketing has also enabled businesses to save on their means of reaching their target market or audience. Through a small fraction of the cost of traditional advertisements, businesses can further allow their customers to conduct research and eventually purchase their products in the most convenient way. This also makes them more appealing to their clients because they can provide results in a very short span of time.

Internet marketing has also allowed these businesses to measure their statistics in a much easier and inexpensive way. Since almost all the aspects of this marketing type can be measured, tested and traced through the use of ad servers, advertisers can easily use and observe their data as to which ads reap the most customer views or purchases. This way, online businesses will be able to determine which of their advertising messages are more appealing to their target customers. The results of all their campaigns can be tracked right away since this marketing initiative simply requires a customer to click the ads, visit a certain website or perform a desired action like filling out a form or purchasing a product or service.

Now as a beginner in the world of internet marketing, you will be responsible for the task of bringing in potential clients by providing them the services or the company that suits their needs or preferences in various internet venues. You will help these customers find the product that they are looking for. The targets are the people who have computers with internet access. Entrepreneurs like you can visit your online store anytime. Consumers can also do the same whenever they want. The future of the world wide web is so bright with its projected online consumer traffic reaching almost 60% and over 80% of these customers shopping online. So if you are determined to make it successful for you, you may just find yourself enjoying the benefits of having an online business that will give you more profit in the long run.

With that said, internet marketing brings you many advantages of incurring minimal costs in starting up your business including cheaper advertising options, a global marketplace, becoming your own boss, promoting stuff that you are passionate about and profiting from these passions along the way. Sounds amazing doesn't it?

Though there are many benefits from internet marketing, it does come with its own share of risks and investments. You must understand that this process will not let you rake in a lot of cash quickly. Your time, diligence, persistence and passion for learning more are very important in your success in internet marketing.

Those who think that this is a get rich quick scheme are bound to be disappointed. Though many businesses have become extremely successful, you will find that those who have failed in this venture have simply wished to become overnight millionaires. The realities of a physical business are still applicable to your online store, including tax payments, customer services and even hiring employees.

Furthermore, it is important that you know that starting an online business is not free. There are costs that may be less than what will be used in building a physical business, but you will still have to shell out for web design, software, hosting, domains and advertising costs. Another reality of having an online business is site downtime. Yes, your site may go down due to technical difficulties or glitches, and this will probably bring a lot of frustration not just on your part but also on the customers' end. Every single minute or second that your site is unavailable to visitors and potential customers, you will be losing money. You need to be prepared for this.

Furthermore, you cannot just rely on a certain system and have it run on autopilot to generate profit. Technology changes and the industry evolves rapidly, making any "autopilot system" that is supposed to generate cash a complete lie. A marketing tactic that worked for someone in the past may not work for you at all in the future. Therefore, it is very important to keep yourself updated with new technologies and marketing trends.

Competition will always be around so if you do not keep yourself informed and you do not work hard, you will not stand out in the crowd. You have to make an impact! Work hard because if not, you can be sure that one of your competitors is out there doing so. Besides, if you want your business to be a long-term investment, your first profits should go back to your site's services and advertising efforts. Maximize your profits and do not just cash out your first earnings. It will also be helpful to learn about taxation and other related laws that affect this industry. This way, you know what your tax and legal advantages are once you set up your business. This will also help in protecting your assets, thus, it should never be overlooked.

With all these realities in mind, you will need to be very determined to stand out in this industry. Internet marketing is not for the person who likes simple routines. You should be flexible in learning new strategies and trends in order to keep up with your competition.

Now that you know what internet marketing is and all the good and bad that comes with it, you will now learn the marketing methods that online businesses have been using in order to promote their services and products to the global marketplace.

The following methods that will be discussed further in the next few passages are:

Affiliate marketing

Article marketing

E-mail marketing

Blog marketing

Pay per click ads or PPC

Search engine optimization or SEO

Pop-up ads

Banner ads

Social media marketing

Mobile marketing

These internet marketing methods are not equal at all. Each of them have strategies to reach a target market and will produce varying results based on your goal, marketing pitch and relationship with your customer. Whether you are going to market your own website or choose to get involved in affiliate marketing, you are most likely going to use a couple of these methods at various times. Remember, what you earn in this industry is always proportionate to all the effort and time you have invested in developing your website.

Now let's proceed to the juicy part of this subject. In the next few pages, you will learn each of the internet marketing methods mentioned above. You will get to know what they are, what they do, how they work and why they are effective.

Affiliate Marketing

Affiliate marketing is an online practice wherein a business rewards an affiliate for the visitors or customers brought in by his marketing efforts. The rewards are either cash or gifts and are given for either an offer completion or site referral. In this process, there are four players – the merchant, network, publisher and customer. Recently, this market has grown complex with the secondary players like affiliate management agencies, third party vendors (specialized) and super-affiliates. It works by simply using the affiliate's website to drive traffic to the merchant's own site or to allow visitors to be forwarded to the merchant's main web page.

Basically, this is also what we can call revenue sharing between the online merchants and online affiliates. The compensation given to the affiliates depend on how many user clicks, sales or registrations were made on the merchant's website via their own. Affiliate marketing enables the automation of the advertising processes and the payment for desired actions. Merchants have preferred this internet marketing strategy because it is a "pay per performance" model, where they do not incur any expenses for marketing their products unless the affiliate produces the results they need.

Affiliate marketing can also be translated as a type of business relationship where you, as an affiliate, promote a merchant's services which is different from yours. This means that you do not need to have your own product in order to venture into affiliate marketing. You only need to promote your business provider's services and products.

This is how it works – you need to have a web page that contains a link that directs your users or visitors to the main page or online store of the merchant. When one of your site visitors clicks on that link and purchases something from the merchant's website, you will get a sort of commission or a referral fee. This way you are the one driving traffic to your merchant's website through your own web page. The merchant will pay you whenever a visitor from your site buys something or signs up for something on their site. A special affiliate link is assigned to your web page, making it easy for the merchant to track customers coming from your site. One merchant is allowed different affiliate links and all of them will direct the users to its website.

Another strategy that works in affiliate marketing is the use of web page codes or web cookies. This is actually a very interesting way to still profit even if your visitor clicks on the affiliate link and does not purchase from the merchant's site at once. How does this work? The moment a user clicks on the link, a cookie is stored in his computer, indicating that he or she visited the merchant's site and recording your page as the one that referred him to that website. If, let's say a couple of weeks later, the user finally decides to buy something from the merchant's online store and types the web address of the merchant directly into his browser, the cookies stored in his computer will still recognize the purchase as a referral from your affiliate link, allowing you to receive a compensation from the merchant. Note that cookies have expiration, so you must read the affiliate program's terms carefully to check the life span of these cookies.

The success of affiliate marketing has also paved way for the rise of many online companies such as Amazon.com, which now has thousands of affiliates.

Article Marketing

Article marketing is an online advertising strategy used by many businesses to market their websites, products or services by writing short articles that are related to their industry. It is the practice of posting these keyword-focused writings on article syndication sites that have a good readership following. These articles will then be distributed and published in the marketplace. Many opine that article marketing is an essential element in any internet marketing strategy. These articles have the intention of providing information and entertainment to online users. Typically these articles have a resource box or bio box that indicates the references and contact information of the writer's business. The resource box may also contain a link back to the website that the author is promoting in order to attract the readers to visit that website.

Articles that are well-researched and written are usually released and distributed for free in order for the business to gain more credibility within the market. Through these articles, a website or online business will be able to attract more new clients. Internet marketers usually submit the articles to several article directories in order to maximize the results of their online campaign. In order to avoid the filtering process of the internet for duplicate content, internet marketers attempt what we call article spinning or article rewriting and rewording to give certain variations to the original article. Through this, the article can acquire site visitors coming from several websites for article directories. Getting your article to be featured in niche blogs or focused content websites that are managed by others is a good and popular strategy in terms of article marketing. If you are a guest blogger on these websites, you will be able to introduce your business to an interested audience that may have been otherwise unreachable.

The common practice in internet publishing is to have your articles use relevant keywords and catchy titles with around 250 to 500 words in the body. If you incorporate the keywords or keyword phrases in your articles, it is possible to get more search engine traffic.

Which, among the hundreds of article directories, should you submit your articles to? This is actually one of the most tedious tasks in this marketing method. Today, businesses and experts usually outsource their article marketing methods including the submission process. The most popular article directories that are recommended include EzineArticles, IdeaMarketers and GoArticles.

Article marketing can also help you generate leads that you can include in your e-mail list. In writing your articles, you must give the readers an offer so irresistible that it will prompt them to visit your website and sign up for your services. Once you have their information, you can start creating a sales-winning partnership with them. Failing to do this will not give you another chance to sell to your leads.

Among the best offers you can give your readers may include quizzes, special reports on a certain topic, free consultation sessions or free book chapters. This way, your readers will be enticed to provide you with their e-mail addresses that you can use to further send marketing news and information about your website.

Overall, the most important factor in article marketing is to get people to visit your website and sign up or purchase one of your services. Writing articles that are accurate, specific and helpful will attract more potential leads or clients.

E-mail Marketing

This is one of the most cost-efficient methods of internet marketing that promotes your business. In order to execute an effective and successful e-mail campaign, you need the right information to achieve your desired results.

E-mail marketing is a direct marketing method that makes use of e-mails to communicate a commercial message to your target market. It is the process of sending messages to your previous or current customers in order to encourage them to do business with you again and in turn enhance your business relationship with them. E-mail marketing is also used to acquire new clients and convince your current customers to buy something at once.

There are several advantages in using this type of internet marketing. For one, almost all internet users have e-mail accounts that they check regularly. With this form of communication, advertisers can easily reach those who have signed up to receive regular communications regarding subjects that interests them. It is cost-effective and has a short impact time.

E-mail marketing can be categorized into three types: direct e-mail, intermediary e-mail and retention e-mail.

Direct e-mail usually is an email message with commercial sales content. They are usually sent to customers who have previously used a certain product or service or to potential clients in your target audience who might enjoy and benefit from the service you are offering. Direct mail marketing may make use of a company's e-mail list or a purchased or shared e-mail list or a list that is acquired from a third party service. These third party services may already know which audience can be target through e-mail marketing or they may conduct an analysis to find out which e-mail addresses will bring the highest conversion or responses for your business.

Retention e-mail or newsletter mail on the other hand, are designed and written for promotional use. They aim to provide a long-term impact to the customer's mind, thus, their content is more than a sales message. The retention mail specifies the benefits of the products or services that a company offers in a more informative format.

Intermediary e-mail is a message sent by a company delegated by the main provider to send out advertising and marketing e-mails to a list of subscribers that is usually owned by the intermediary company.

In order to be successful in e-mail marketing, you must always use all relevant information that is necessary for your business. You may send messages to your customers if you find that they will benefit from what you are about to offer them. In sending these e-mails, you must also write an informative and straight forward headline in order to grab your customer's attention. Before sending out your e-mail, check the message and use both text and HTML formats to make sure that your message will be received and read, or you may include options to view your mail in these formats.

Blog Marketing

Blogs have become one of the useful platforms for internet marketing. Subscribers of a blog usually sign up to receive content on a regular basis and since most subscribers remain loyal when they receive relevant and useful information, a strong following and readership will be a good way to reach these potential customers and get them to either sign up or purchase a service from your business. Blogs have continuously reached their targets most of the time, making them a very effective way to market one's services or products.

Blog marketing, as the name suggests, is done via a web blog through a series of weekly or daily posts about a certain topic. A lot of businesses have used blogs to communicate and interact with their customers while featuring their services. Organizations have also used blogs to share and review a product's features and benefits prior to their official launch. They also pave way for companies to gather or receive feedback from the consumers in order to confirm if their services and products meet the expectations of their clients.

Since blog marketing focuses on interaction with online users, you may also start blogging in order to market your product line to get more exposure to the cyber market.

However, you will have to write and design a blog that will stand out from your competitors. This way, your blog will also gain more popularity, making more websites want to link to it. The more websites linking to your blog, the more traffic and profit you will get. You must always remember to give your audience or target subscribers a reason to always visit your blog. If your subscriber leaves any comments, be sure to send them a thank you e-mail. Hold small contests every now and then where you can give away discounts and coupons to your subscribers. You may also ask your followers to post the link of your blog to their own websites in exchange for free product samples.

Pay-per-click or PPC

PPC or Pay-per-click advertisements, also known as Cost Per Click, are used to bring in traffic to websites where advertisers provide compensation to the hosting site whenever their ad is clicked. There are two models for determining how much is to be paid per click – flat-rate and bid-based rate. In both models, advertisers consider the value of a click from a certain source where such value depends on the type of customer that the company is targeting and what can be gained from his or her visit (which is usually revenue).

If you currently have a running website or a blog and would like to earn extra profit, you can try this internet marketing method. Put in pay-per-click ads on your blog or web page and merchants will pay you a percentage every time your visitors click on them.

One of the most popular PPC is Google Adsense. It is very easy to add this to your blog and more so if you use Blogger which is also managed by Google. Adsense displays a number of advertisements that target a specific audience on your blog. In order to sign up for pay-per-click ads like Google Adsense, you will need to complete an online form as your official application.

Search Engine Optimization (SEO)

Whenever you search for a topic on Google, Yahoo or MSN, you usually get pages and pages of websites that have the keywords you typed in the search bar. Have you ever wondered why a particular website is listed first on the results of your search? The primary reason for this is Search Engine Optimization.

Search engine optimization allows a website to become search engine friendly, making it rank higher on search results compared to other websites that have the same keyword contents. Usually, these search engines read and archive sites regularly so that they can be found easily whenever a search is performed by a user. For example, if a user types in "parenting" in the search bar and your website is about the same topic and is optimized properly, your website will appear in the first page of the search results.

Basically, SEO makes your website easier for these search engines to understand. Its goal is to increase your website's rank in the search results that will in turn bring in more traffic to your site. Remember, the more traffic you get, the more potential for profit you will have.

On-site and off-site factors are the ones that can determine your search engine rankings. On-site factors include your page content and your title heading. Off-site factors like pages that link to your site, words used to link to your page and how long such link has existed also come into play. It is important that you focus on your site's SEO continuously because if you get good search engine rankings consistently, you will always have free traffic.

Pop-up Ads

During your internet surfing time, you probably have come across many of these pop-up ads. These are advertisement windows that appear once you visit a website. Their aim is to generate traffic or simple capture your e-mail address.

Many people have found this internet marketing method quite annoying since it disrupts them from getting information from the website they are viewing. However, these ads, intrusive as they have been tagged, also have certain advantages. For one, they are much more effective than banner ads. They pull up a 15% click through rate while the banners only yield a mere 3%. Pop-up ads also are effective and gives a click through percentage of 6.5. Since they are more effective than banner ads, they also cost you a lot more. However, the return on investment with the use of these ads is much higher. Furthermore, when this ad is the only window on the page, there will be no other images that will conflict with the brand that you are selling.

In the recent years though, these advertising methods have become less popular due to the development of pop-up blockers.

✓ Banner Ads

A banner ad is basically a graphic, text or an image displayed on websites that aim to promote a company's product or service. They are actually small HTML codes, but their importance in internet marketing and business is significant. Banner ads vary in sizes and orientation but will often come in rectangular shape and are 486 x 60 pixels high (full banner). There is actually no universal rule when it comes to banner ad file sizes, but the size will still depend on the website where it will be displayed. These sites impose certain limits to banner sizes since it adds up to the total size of the web page they are displayed on, thereby resulting to more waiting times while the page loads on a browser.

Due to the banner ads' graphic elements, you may find these ads somehow similar to those you see in printed media such as magazines and newspapers. However, these banner ads have the ability to direct the user to the advertiser's main web page. If you are interested in displaying or posting a banner on a certain website, you can arrange with the publisher to have your banner posted or pay a banner network to post the ad on a number of websites. You may also arrange with the publisher to simply display their ads on your site in exchange for them displaying your banner ads.

Social Media Marketing

Social media marketing is basically the process of marketing your business through social media portals such as Facebook, YouTube and Twitter. This allows for businesses to have a more personal and dynamic interaction and connection with their clients and potential customers.

Strategies in social media marketing can be as simple as maintaining a blog, a Facebook or Twitter account or attaching "tweet this" icons to the end of your articles or ads. It can also be as complex as having a full campaign that includes blogging, social networking, tweeting and spreading viral videos.

As marketing is the process of informing consumers what your business is, who you are and what your products are, social media further helps in introducing your business to a global network of possible customers. The use of social media to prove a business' identity and to create business relationships with people who do not have the chance be aware of your products and services is a highly recommended option in internet marketing. Moreover, it is an avenue that can be accessed by anyone who has an internet connection and is an inexpensive way to implement your marketing strategies and business campaigns.

Mobile Marketing

Mobile marketing has been a concept that has attained various definitions. It is primarily described to be the marketing strategy that makes use of mobile media to communicate with a target market. Recently a more updated definition was given by the Mobile Marketing Association, saying that mobile marketing is actually a combination of practices that gives organizations the ability to engage, communicate and interact with their audience through a mobile device or network.

The most popular mobile device used for this is a cell-phone. To use this medium, you will need to set up a short code and have your customers register to receive your SMS or text messages. Mobile optimization will also make sure that your website is displayed correctly on a mobile phone browser. Search engine optimization has undergone many changes that made internet marketers become more interested in the mobile version of their optimized websites compared to the traditional website optimization. Most mobile phones today have internet access or wireless capabilities. These devices have provided more flexibility on both the business' and consumer's ends in terms of receiving and sending data related to the products or services which a company offers.

The most typical types of mobile marketing include the use of MMS or Multimedia Messaging Service, Bluetooth technology, Infrared and Mobile Internet. Marketing through a mobile device is now a trend in many developed countries where almost every one has a mobile phone. This is also a more cost-effective method of promoting your

business and is much easier for most age groups to understand. More time is now spent online with the use of these devices, making your business available to consumers who are always on the go and would still want to receive updates from your end.

In MMS mobile marketing, a slideshow of text and images that may include a video or audio is a perfect way to capture a potential customer's attention effectively. The ad is delivered via MMS. The use of Bluetooth technology in marketing makes use of radio based frequencies to transfer data on higher speeds. Infrared, on the other hand, is a bit limited, as its frequency range only reaches as far as 1 meter.

Mobile marketing is a new way to ensure customer awareness and boost your sales. With all the new smart phones, tablets and modern mobile devices, mobile marketing is definitely destined to progress in the years to come.

All the major internet marketing methods have been discussed in detail in this guide. It is now up to you to choose which one you prefer, however, remember the things that you need to have in order to succeed – good research, a positive mindset and attitude, diligence, patience and focus. All the best.

www.ingramcontent.com/pod-product-compliance
Lightning Source LLC
Chambersburg PA
CBHW051714170526
45167CB00002B/659